So *YOU* want to be a

Professional

ATHLETE

So *YOU* want to be a
Professional
ATHLETE

A GUIDE FOR
RAISING, BEING AND COACHING
THE WORLDS NEXT SUPERSTAR

BY RORY T. EDWARDS

Published by:
Professional Woman Publishing
www.pwnbooks.com

ISBN: 978-0-9961889-6-8

Contents

Foreword

Before embarking upon the writing of the foreword for this book, I did some reflecting on the meaning and purpose of a book foreword. A foreword is a word before the word; it is a message before the message. A message needs to be very important to require a message just to tell you that it is coming. John the Baptist came to tell people that Jesus was on the way. He let the people know that they needed to get ready for what was coming next.

The more I reflected on the foreword for this book I concluded that my message should be to get you, the reader, ready for the message that follows. I concluded that the best way to do that was by emphasizing the importance of the message and the qualifications of the person delivering it.

The message in this book is about the most important responsibility parents and caring adults have, which is to prepare the next generation to be responsible parents and caring adults. One of the areas through which we do that preparing is sports. When done properly, sports can be the avenue through which we teach some of life's greatest lessons, instill some of its most cherished values, form some of its most endearing and enduring relationships, and have our greatest fun. When done improperly, sports can be the avenue through which adults inflict upon young people their greatest frustrations, most painful losses, deepest humiliations, and most crushing embarrassments; while setting them up for life long failure.

Rory Edwards has seen all of the above. He worked with his own children and has worked with Athletes since his own athletic days. When Rory Edwards asked me to write the foreword for this book, I do not think he knew how important this subject was to me and how connected I was to it. He knew that I was, and am deeply concerned about young people, and have worked with them all of my adult life. I met Rory in that capacity. However, I do not think he knew how similar our backgrounds were in relationship to sports, and the role sports have played in both of our lives.

As was Rory, I too was an outstanding athlete. My best sport was baseball. I was the center fielder on my high school team that won state championship my junior and senior years. I was in the first group of athletes Jackson State University gave scholarships to play baseball. After an outstanding college career, I tuned down the opportunity to pursue baseball as a profession, but continued to love and play sports for fun well into my fifties. Sports have been a source of life long fun for me and the avenue through which I have connected with so many young people and made lasting friendships. To this day, some of my closest friends and longest friendships are with people I played sports with. However, I never coached a sport.

Rory Edwards, in addition to playing sports and being very good at them, has coached for many years. In his role as coach, he worked with athletes and their parents. In this work, he has learned some very valuable lessons about effectively working with young people to develop them into the productive, healthy adults we want them to become.

Both Rory and I have seen what athletics can do for children; and what it can do to them. Both of us want to see them experience the good and avoid the bad. In his working with young people and their parents over the last three decades, Rory developed a roadmap that will lead to the goals parents want for their athletes and will avoid the pitfalls they don't want.

The information Rory is providing in this book is precious. It is precious because it is about the most precious gifts we have, our children. I have read the material that follows and can assure you that it is very valuable and accurate information. It is life changing information. In a way, it is even life-saving information.

In this book, we have a coach using knowledge he gained about life through coaching to coach parents, coaches and athletes into becoming better coaches for their children in sports and in life. In the end, this book is about the game of life. The world is the playing field or the court. How successful we are in life is often determined by how well we play the game; and how well we play the game is often determined by the quality of our coaching. Those who read this book and take heed to its message will be far better coaches and the children they work with are likely to have far better lives.

I believe that every parent wants his or her child to be a star. Unfortunately, many insist on stardom in the wrong places. Every child has the potential of stardom, if not in athletics, at least in whatever God has given him/her gifts in being. And God has given them all gifts. It is up to parents and other caring adults to nurture those gifts so that every child will shine. The information that follows will improve your coaching, parenting and playing ability and improve the chances that every child you influence will become a Star.

Professor William Jenkins

Acknowledgements

I Would Like to Humbly Acknowledge My Parents, (late) Richard Sr. and Janice Edwards who's unconditional love and support, inspired me to never settle for not achieving my best. To my grandmother, Iola Choice who showed me through her actions and words, that anything you desired and deserved you could overcome. To my brother, Richard, thanks for being my hero. To my sister Jan, who never allowed me to procrastinate. To my Aunt Jean who showed me how to live life on your own terms. To the (late) Willie Banks, my Godmother who unlocked the voice in me. To my cousin, the (late) Roland Williams, who believed in me sometimes more than I did in myself? To the reason I rise every day, the heartbeat of my existence, my amazing children, Rick, Sharde & Aja, who have also blessed me with (4) absolutely awesome grandchildren, Ricky Jr. Saniah, Leah & Hayden.

I would like to express my deepest affection and appreciation, to my life-long and true family of brothers and sisters, Jerry Artis, Stephen Johnson, Valerie Ingram, Daphne Majors, Marcus Stevenson, (late) Eric Echols, Pauline Davis, Tony, McQuiller, (late) Winslow Jennings, Mark and Sandra Jackson Sr., Brian (Homer) Walden, Sheila Robinson, Garfield Duckett, Rodney & Terre (twin) Roberts, NBHS Track & Field Family, Brothers of "FAMILY", Nellis (AFB) Family and my GTA Family.

To the many friends and family who have traveled this journey with me for a reason, a season or a lifetime I applaud and thank you for your contribution.

To the thousands of young people, who call me (Step) Dad, Uncle or just Mr. Rory, Mr. Edwards or Big Bruh, I thank you and love you for allowing me the opportunity to plant a seed of your true value to the world in your life.

To three men who have given me guidance and direction in this journey, Dr. Charles Mate-Kole, Professor William Jenkins and The great liberator Dr. John Carlos. I thank you for believing in me.

Finally yet importantly, to the person who gave me the opportunity to believe in LOVE!! I Thank You my Dream Girl -12/22

Introduction

As a Father, Grandfather, Community Activist, Educator, Entre-preneur, Sports Coach, Consultant, Inspirational Speaker and LIFE COACH. I have been very interested and researched, how children and adults understand and respond to misfortune in their lives. I confidently believe that one's response to failure or to the possibility of failure is a strong indication of a person's internal sense of self-worth and feelings of competence. The tightrope that parents of potential or current sporting phenom-enon's have to walk between encouraging their child to fulfill their potential and pushing them too far possibly to the thresh-old of damaging their mental or physical health is the purpose of this guide.

All across America in too many households' sports and enter-tainment have been much the focus of many of our children. Many of them have unrealistic dreams of becoming professional athletes. Rather than seeing, hearing and watching the rags-to-riches stories where underprivileged athletes reach the Promised Land by way of their talents, the undeniable stories are of the many who never make it, which resonates deeper in the fabric of America than most want to admit. What about the athlete who has two parents, lived in the suburbs or projects, had hall of fame credentials, went to private schools and were told their entire life they would play at the highest level? The road to athletic stardom is more difficult than many imagine and only a precious, lucky few will ever complete the journey. It would help parents, coaches and their children to know early what their chances are of becoming one of the lucky few.

In this book, I hope to impart some real experiences, exercises and a blueprint that can help you reach your full potential but also information that will help you accept the fact that athletics are not the only path there is for a worthwhile and wonderful life. You can become greater than you ever imagined even if you do not make it as a professional athlete. Many parents and athletes themselves are in denial and believe they have the next superstar right at the end of the hallway in their house or next door, when the true essence of achieving that pinnacle of Professional Athletics is so much more than belief and being the fastest on the street from telephone pole to telephone pole. The "So You Want to Be a Professional Athlete" guide will take you through every phase of development, and show you how to recognize the signs of your child becoming the next Lebron James, Mariel Margaret Hamm-Garciaparra (Mia Hamm), Peyton Manning, Cam Newton, Jackie Robinson, Derrick Jeter, Skylar Diggins, Pele, Commissioner of the NFL, NBA, MLB, NHL or President of the United States of America.

What does sports mean to America and Americans?

Sports are a significant part of the American culture, and that should not be taken for granted or deemed unimportant. It is a privilege to be able to play professional sports and enjoy cheering and watching those who have achieved this prestige pinnacle, but for athletes throughout America who engage in sports, many times it is an escape from the pressure of life. From the time a young athlete puts on a helmet and shoulder pads, scores his first basket, hits his first home run or scores his first goal, the dream of playing professional sports resonates in their mind.

In America, there are two types of athletes: Spontaneous and Serious.

Our goal is to evolve the serious athlete's commitment to continue adding a brick a day, to building his/her empire by lifelong awards and nurturing of your most valued investment (You). Through this, your empire can mature and be prepared to provide resources to you and your family when your playing days are well over. Our goal is for your '*Lifestyles Management Preparation*' to provide you with the mindset to live your current life or at least your current dreams, for the remainder of your life. Understanding the dynamics of this transformation period, will determine the size of your kingdom.

CHAPTER 1

Being truthful early with yourself and your child about their ability

One of the greatest joys of being an adult is becoming a parent. I often think about the experience of watching my children being born and wondering in awe about that process. From your first glance of this miraculous development, your mind goes into over-drive about all the things you want to do and make sure they experience all that you may not have had the opportunity to fulfill. In many homes, sports is one of the first things that is brought to the forefront. Many years ago comedian Robin Harris made a joke about a woman he dated with multiple children and he took them in the backyard to see which one had some type of athletic ability and concluded they were just Be-Be kids. This statement has stretched across the nation in how some people identify misbehaving children and how imperative sports are to many. In several cases, parents generally are the worst judges of their child's true ability. The emotional invest-ment clouds judgment and blinds parents from seeing their child may not be gifted in sports. Instead of identifying this lack of ability, some parents push harder and end up pushing their child too far. When children who lack ability are forced to compete, they are often placed in humiliating situations where they continually fail. Instead of cultivating healthy self-esteem from sports participation, the repeated embarrassment can cause the child to become stressed, anxious, withdrawn and depressed. The child also may develop a negative sense of self due to the poor performances, instead of looking to character traits, actions and other abilities to build healthy self-esteem.

As a youth basketball coach, I can recall the many times I would have parents who wanted their child to be a part of my team because of the success the team had in the previous seasons. One of the hardest things to explain to a parent is their child is really not ready to compete on a level for which you believe they are. In one of my earlier seasons of coaching, I recall a conversation with a mother of a younger player who felt her son could make a major contribution to the team since his father was a former NBA player. He had the DNA to play and her observations of his ability to make some impressive shots in their yard was her justification for him being a member of this team. This is her story: This spring I let my son join the church league youth basketball because basketball and Coach Edwards **are** the only sport that will give him a chance. Therefore I said "why not, it should be fun, right?" Since I was new to the whole sports mom approach I went in with such optimism that it clearly made me stand out from the other seasoned sports mom's. The first couple of games I was optimistic and excited, shouting positively and respectfully for my son's team and the competitors. As the season started, I noticed my son's efforts to play the sport were there but compared to the experience of other kids they were unwillingly making him look as if he was not even trying to play. The look on his face every time he missed the shot, or when he tried to out run kids who were clearly more athletic and mature than him was breaking my heart. I believe as a mother, we try to protect our children from everything that might hurt them, including bad feelings. I started questioning myself, was I being too protective? Or was it just my motherly instinct of not wanting my child to fail? But as the weeks went by I noticed that the emphasis on winning was giving me anxiety. I felt as if I could not breathe; it seemed that the optimism that I brought in was clearly fading, quickly. So then I asked myself, why was I so emotionally involved in this? The reason I let him join the church league basketball team was so we could spend time together as a family, and for him to try it to see if he liked playing the sport or not. I quickly came to my senses; I thought to myself, does this anxiety come from me wanting to fit in the community, or please the other parents, or giving me an opportunity to tell people his father played in the NBA? Am I feeling this way because my son is not as athletic as I would want him to be, or is this coming from me not wanting him to fail at anything? I made myself a promise and to help keep the keep promise I made a list of things to think about that would help me get through the season without having a nervous breakdown. Some might sound as a cliché to the normal person, but I am far from normal so they worked in my case. I had to realize the truth, did I want this more for my son than he wanted at this time? Or since his father was not in my life, would my son's NBA career fill that void of me and his father never living out the NBA wife and husband dream? This is just one story among many conversations which happens in families who are looking for the quick dollar opportunity. It is like the family who calls each other to share one special number with hopes of winning the lottery. The chances are slim of winning the lottery just as they are for your child signing a professional sports contract. It will take commitment, sacrifice, timing and favor. The truth is one's talent which many have, has helped many live out life-long dreams of what if. But, what if not? What is your secondary plan (A)? Because a plan (B) means you did not believe in your plan (A) when you created it.

Activity: Truthfully rate you or your childs ability in these areas

Strengths of Ability (1-5)	Weakness of Ability (1-5)
Talent / Athleticism	
Commitment	
Work Ethic	
Confidence and Leadership	
Ability to Learn and Improve	
Your dream or theirs	
Total	Total

CHAPTER 2

Make academics a
priority over the sport

How many times have you heard from athletes the statement, "School is not cool?" "I only stayed in because of sports". It usually comes out of the mouth of someone who did not have a successful passage in school and can share all the reasons why he/she did not make it. They have no plan to share why they should have made it, but the system failed them. Dreams of multi-million-dollar contracts, Olympic triumph, huge endorsement contracts and college scholarships have many parents pushing their children harder than ever to play sports. Children are being entered into sports leagues at much younger ages, and in most cases not developmentally mature enough to understand the philosophy of the sport. Some are pushed to participate year-round in as many sports as parents can sign them up for, with the hopes of creating the next superstar. Many are forced to let their parents live vicariously through their dreams of stardom by the child's participation in sports, rather than for the child's benefit. Involving your child in sports has many positive benefits. However, persuading children into playing sports because it can develop them into coping with life much better later on, can negatively impact their emotional development and damage the parent-child bond.

All across this nation, especially in urban America, we have millions of young men and women who aspire, dream and put in overtime to be called a professional athlete. However, out of those millions, we know that very few will make it. At the same time, we have millions who are dropping out of school, and very few address this concern with the same vigor as those who address angrily the elimination of extracurricular sports in school or mandatory study hall for failing athletes. I'm reminded daily as I watch young men and women commit to a school they have no idea of what the end results will be. They have no idea what is in store for them but in conversation about the future, they have that gleam in their eye of one day playing a professional sport. However, school in many cases has been looked upon as unnecessary or just getting in the way of them fulfilling their dream. The reality of fulfillment comes from one factor. If they are uneducated and unprepared mentally, socially and physically, there will be great disappointment at the end of this journey, and this is why I wanted to write this book. I recall a position that I was engrossed in as NAACP President of The New Britain Connecticut Chapter, several years ago regarding if students who were academically ineligible or in jeopardy of failing. Should they still be able to participate in any extracurricular activities unless they had received a grade of (C) or above? My stance was they should not!! Why? First, NCAA regulations would not allow you to participate on the collegiate level and second, you are allowing the student to be set up for failure in life, if they are incapable through their emotional intelligence to compete on the stage of life after sports. This was met with much resistance, especially from those I expected would support my stance based on their child ever having a chance to leave the community would come down to that child being academically eligible to play college sports would ride on them obtaining a (C) grade or better. Their resistance grew in numbers from meeting to meeting, to the request of this mandate being presented to our local school board. Many non-supporters of this proposal such as athletes, parents, school administrators, coaches and former superstars, took their concerns to the local newspapers stating I was being inconsiderate to the fact that many of the children who would be affected by this mandate were only in school to participate in sports and if that was taken away from them, they might drop out or end up on the wrong side of the law. Some even had the audacity to state I was just jealous of the possibilities their child may have through the avenue of sports. Well, not to make this about me, but my athletic resume was one of the best the city has ever experienced, but it was the fact that I could comprehend and pass the SAT is what got me a college scholarship, not just my talent. This debate went on for about six months at the many bi-weekly, board of education meetings, in the barbershops, hair salons, in the pulpit of the churches, on the streets of the city and even at my own NAACP meetings. Many believed I had lost my direction and rather than helping the citizens of the city as I pledged to do, I was using the position as NAACP President to advance my own agenda. So, on that monumental day of the board's vote I was out-numbered at least (30) against to (1) for, as the board members asked for final comments on why they should vote one way or another. I still recall the verbal assassination of my reasoning. The twenty-five minutes for the board deliberation seemed like days, but they returned with the vote for the rule but lowered it to a (C-) They concluded they would gradually increase the standards over time. I thanked them for having the courage to allow our children a chance at life for a lifetime, not a season. However, left them with the thought of what would the NCAA change to allow your student to compete? In the movie "Coach Carter," he showcased a great example of the following: If you give individuals and or athletes the resources to learn, they will sense they are normally intelligent people and with structure and guidance they will adhere to any challenges put before them. However, because their parents were convinced their athletic abilities would have gotten them to the Promise Land, education and proper behavior are not and were not sufficiently stressed. The NCAA has quietly implemented several propositions and roadblocks for the talented ten to just play; today, you must know how to read or turn in your playbook.

I often remind myself, and those who do not believe it, that to be a successful athlete you must first become an intelligent human being. Many times, we live vicariously through our children's success, only to execute our failures once again. The road to becoming a professional athlete is 10,000 times more difficult than becoming an esteemed scholar. A wise man once shared with me that if he was to remove me of all of my worldly possessions, the one thing he could never ever take is my wisdom or acquired knowledge.

Our priorities have shifted to making the quick dollar, lotto, pro-sports, entertainment, get rich quick schemes and illegal activities. But the odds of having long term success with any of those things is imprudent thinking. Successful people I have spoken to have shared their road having the never-giving-up spirit no matter how hard or tough the journey has been. They professed their commitment to working multiple hours, days or years at perfecting the craft. They shared that when you replace hard work with excuses you get exactly what excuses are; they are tools of the incompetent used to build monuments to nothing. For those who specialize in them shall never be good at anything else. There is a saying I use that states, "The reputation of a thousand years may be determined **(destroyed)** by the conduct of one hour." We must provide our young citizens with as much information and resources as possible to not only compete for a professional roster spot, but to compete for a spot in this global market of competition of wealth distribution.

Activity: Develop your sports resume and personal resume side by side

JOHN DOE

100 River Road, New York, NY 10000
555.555.5555 (Res), 555.666.6666 (Cell), rudy@aol.com

SENIOR EXECUTIVE

15 years successful experience providing fiscal, strategic and operations leadership in uniquely challenging situations

Dynamic, results-oriented leader with a strong track record of performance in turnaround and high-paced organizations. Utilize keen analysis and insights and team approach to drive organizational improvements and implementation of best practices. Superior interpersonal skills, capable of resolving multiple and complex (sales, human resources, legal, financial, operational) issues and motivating staff to peak performance. Excellent political connections developed as selected member of Fiorello LaGuardia's mayoral team. Additional areas of expertise include:

Strategy, Vision & Mission Planning	*Finance, Budgeting & Cost Management*
Sales & Marketing Leadership	*Public Relations & Media Affairs*
Profitability & Cost Analysis	*Policy & Procedure Development*
Programs, Services & Products	*Government Regulations & Relations*
Billing, Collections & Cash Management	*Human Resources Management*
Contract Negotiations & Strategic Alliances	*Team Building & Performance Improvement*

9

PROFESSIONAL EXPERIENCE

NJ STATE SENATE CAMPAIGN, 2002

Led grass-roots Republican campaign and garnered 35% of vote in predominantly Democratic district. Maintained positive campaign with hundreds of volunteers and no paid staff. Ran against incumbent who had been in office 8 years.

Earned endorsement from Mayor, local newspaper, Democratic District Leaders and Democratic clubs in Brooklyn. Endorsed by 17 Democratic ministers.

Exhibited tireless energy, positive attitude and visionary leadership.

PRESIDENT/CEO, 1996 – 2002
UNITED NATIONS DEVELOPMENT CORPORATION, NEW YORK, NY

President and CEO of $250 million NYS public health benefit corporation that controls and develops more than 1 million square feet of commercial and residential property in midtown Manhattan near the United Nations. Served on the cabinet of Mayor Fiorella LaGuardia and acted as his surrogate at various public functions. Accountable for staff of 356 FTEs Managed through 6 direct reports. Provided fiscal, strategic and operational leadership to reduce indebtedness and improve operating results. Revamped internal procedures and controls, reorganized/reallocated staff and implemented best practices and performance monitoring systems in support of Continuous Improvement.

Notable Accomplishments

Withdrew sale of underperforming UN Plaza Hotel from market, repackaged property and successfully sold hotel for $100+million - more than double original expectations and representing one of the largest privatization projects in the city and State of New York.

Sold 300,000 square feet of Class A commercial condominium space for $60 million.

Negotiated and secured a lease extension with the United Nations for more than 600,000 square feet of office space, ensuring the UN's presence in New York City for the next 25 years.

Reduced corporate indebtedness by 30% and maintained A bond rating.

Worked in conjunction with NYC Economic Development Corporation and issued $160M in refunding two new General Obligation bond offerings.

Increased Gross revenues by $80M through rent escalation charges. Improved cash collections reducing DSO (Days Sales Outstanding) by 50%.

COMMISSIONER / CEO, 1994 – 1996
CITY OF NEWARK, DEPARTMENT OF YOUTH SERVICES, NEWARK, NJ

As member of Mayor's cabinet, managed major city agency overseeing the funding and operations of 850 community-based organizations serving over 1 million inner-city youths. Developed and tracked $150 million budget. Challenged to turnaround troubled agency to improve performance and reduce funding requirements. Led a private-sector approach to operations driving accountability and utilization of proven business practices.

Notable Accomplishments

Revamped entire department bringing in all new Commissioner. Redesigned internal procedures and controls to track contract development and vendor payments. Established Key Performance Indicators for all operating departments. Introduced numerous managerial/operational improvements including computerized production of backlog reports, staff cross-training and resource redeployment.

Conducted internal audits to identify systemic problems. Personally visited and evaluated majority of programs eliminating poor performers. Assigned accountability to each Deputy Commissioner/ Director for quality and to ensure adherence to new standards and policies.

Setup new agency payment processing system to tighten cash management and reduced payments from 90 to 5 days allowing all agencies to continue operations without disruption.

Significantly enhanced the RFP process raising the bar on agency standards and qualifications and developing better qualified pool of Community Based Organizations.

Initiated first-ever "City Serve Awards" providing recognition and motivation to youth service participants.

ASSISTANT VICE PRESIDENT / OPERATIONS MANAGER, 1986 – 1994
CHEMICAL BANK, NEW YORK, NY

Assigned to currency processing group, overseeing portfolio in excess of $3 billion. Challenged to eliminate departmental losses stemming from excess costs and process inefficiencies. Documented work procedures for every job. Initiated cross training and employee development. Demonstrated strong interpersonal skills; worked with all levels of staff to understand processes and provide leadership, recognition and motivation.

Notable Accomplishments

Turned results from $300K loss to $50K loss in first year.

Performed complete audit of internal processes diagramming all business workflows. Eliminated redundant positions and outsourced specialty functions. Instituted part-time college student program allowing move from 2-shift to 3-shift operation while reducing costs and FTEs. Slashed turnaround time from seven days to one.

Creatively reduced currency processing time by eliminating physical verification of $1/$5 bundles based on realization that small adjustments were less costly than time incurred to verify.

Conceptualized and implemented creative and compelling marketing program that increased revenues by 20%.

EDUCATION

Harvard University, BS in Economics

BOARDS & MEMBERSHIPS (partial listing)

Board of Trustees, City University of New York, Chair Faculty Staff Administration Committee

Board of Directors, Richmond County Savings Bank Foundation

Board of Directors, Staten Island Community Televisions, Former President

Former President, NAACP Staten Island, Increased membership 300% in one year

Former Board Member, Society for Seamen's Children

Former Board Member and Finance Committee Chair, Christ United Methodist Church

Board of Directors, State Island University Hospital

Former Member, Staten Island YMCA Committee on Management

HONORS & AWARDS
(Recipient of more than 100 honors - partial listing)

Man of the Millennium, Staten Island Friends for Hospice Care

Dr. Martin Luther King Jr. Humanitarian/Brotherhood Award

New York Governor's Award, African Americans of Achievement

African American Leader in New York City Award, Wagner College

Outstanding Community Service Award, Public School 57

Leadership Award, Chemical Bank

Distinguished Community Service Award, YMCA

President's Medal of Honor, College of Staten Island

Leadership Award, Staten Island Branch NAACP

Commitment to Youth Award, MS 158 Beacon Program

13

CHAPTER 3

Invest in your child's success like your Life depends on the result

If life could be a fairy tale story and you had one wish for your child's life, what would that wish be? There are many alternative methods for investing in your child, and sports is just one of many for parents to discover the multiple talents their child may possess. As projected by the US Census Bureau, our communities, urban, suburban and rural communities alike, have become more diverse than ever before. One thing that remains constant among the myriad of youth (and not so youthful often times) in these diverse communities is an affinity for sports. Active involvement in sports can transcend cultural barriers and act as a potential springboard to a professional career for a select group of talented individuals. Accessible public spaces for sport-play to commence, and sportsmanship to be learned, can also offer any community a significant and viable economic boost if managed and supported effectively. Each child learns and develops at different stages. Our brand of skill development provides just this type of sports-based community development to succeed not only in sports but also in life. One of our goals is to ensure the next generation of sportsmen and women are counseled, directed and supported, onto a pathway of fun and success. This means ensuring that communities from urban to rural are provided the proper resources in which people can become conscious of the value of the sports culture, develop skills, and aspire to excellence both academically as well as athletically.

One of my most difficult decisions in my life was to choose academics over the athletics for my son who loved football and in which he was extremely gifted. In his final semester of middle school he brought home his report card which always displayed (A's) and (B's) but this final semester he brought home a (D) which was accompanied by all (A's). In the eye of public opinion, one would say, come on, one (D); give him a break. You brought home (D's). But since I understood what kind of life he would have if he didn't perform at his highest level, I chose the lesson of making him aware that he had lost focus on the larger picture, visualizing the outcome and the rewards. His talent on the field and in the classroom were in balance but this one mistake was not acceptable in one who could have obtained an (A) in this subject like all others, in his sleep. This showed me a lack of focus necessary for *excellence*. I was harshly criticized for my decision from coaches, family members, boosters club and parents of other future players, because in the words of those who wish to utilize his physical talent, he was a *beast* at running back. I responded that he'll be much more than any one play or game could ever define, but this is what helped my decision:

⊙ A young black male in America is more likely to die from gunfire than was any soldier in Vietnam.

⊙ Studies show black male achievement begins to decline as early as the fourth grade and by high school, black males are more likely to drop out; in 2011, only 38.8 percent graduated from high school, compared to 70.8 percent for their white counterparts and 92.6 percent for their Asian counterparts.

For that entire summer, I went back and forth with my decision; was I right or was I being too hard? After that semester, he was back on track as if he had never missed a beat and I told him the football field awaits him, to which he replied: "I lost that fire and will play basketball instead." To this day I question that decision as I counsel young aspiring athletes who are determined to be that 0.03-0.08% that actually make it and then end up the 80% in some type of financial hardship 5-7 years after their last game. Based on studies over the past 15 years and on the testimonials of former players, escaping unscathed is virtually impossible. Nearly two-thirds suffer an injury serious enough to require surgery or sideline them half the season or more. In addition, six of every 10 players suffer a concussion; more than a quarter will suffer more than one, and the odds are that any player who suffers a concussion will later experience headaches, head trauma and serious memory problems. Nearly half of all players retire from football because of an injury. Do I regret my decision? Should I? Will you? My son is a successful businessman, father, college graduate, and most of all, he has never said it, but I believe he knows my only concern was his transformation into greatness.

If you and your family are determined you want your child to be a professional athlete, here are some starter kit conversation topics to have as you progress through this transformation.

Here are five conversation topics to have with yourself and your child

1   Are we as a family prepared to support this transformation of our child into greatness? How does that look, feel and taste?

2   How do we prepare for the long-term misfortune of not making it, or not achieving based on your expectations at the highest level when you get there? (Which may not be the most popular conversation.)

3   When does the conversation of understanding how and when to renew your concentration, determination, purpose begin?

4   Realizing the power of liked minds and knowledge, you cannot get your child to somewhere you have never been.

5   Visualizing, planning and execution of the outcome and the rewards.

CHAPTER 4

Seek a professional trainer that can enhance your child's ability

I always wanted to learn how to play the piano, so people told me the IPad could teach me. What I found out is that the IPad can teach them, but I needed a piano teacher. Both parents and coaches need to understand their different roles. While parents are ultimately responsible for their child's development, once they have selected a coach, they must leave the coaching to that person. Although many parents often recreate with their child, they must resist coaching "over the shoulder" of the coach and/or publicly questioning the coaches decisions. Why is this so important to the development of your child? As humans, the success of our child is a reflection of our ability to nurture. Wrong! Your parenting evaluation is not based on your child's success in athletics, it is based on their choices to be great in whatever they do but also understanding the process of the journey, through your teachings not you enabling them.

Is This the Right Choice or Is the Parent the First Coach and best Choice?

Many parents have played the game at the highest level, but when you are playing, it does not always mean that you will be an amazing coach when your playing days are over. It is how serious were you about the preparation and learning process when playing. Many have said they were the best to ever do it, but I remember hearing when I was a child, there is someone out there who is bigger, faster, tougher, smarter and stronger who wants it just as bad as you do. While providing professional training may not be the answer for everyone's children, many will benefit greatly from having the advantage of someone who offers this benefit. Not only will your children learn new skills which can help them understand healthy living for the rest of their lives, but also they will begin to see accomplishments almost immediately. When you understand the up side to how it may be beneficial to you and your child, it can take a lot of pressure off the timeline of your desired success and let the process take its course. Because they will be working with someone who has been professionally trained in sports training and aware of the most modern techniques, their risks of injury is decreased.

Activity

Here are five criteria's you should evaluate / score your coach on when selecting or training to become a professional.

Score each category on a scale of (1-20)

I   **Patience –** How patient is the coach in teaching past learning, failure and success?

----

2   **Communication –** Your coach likely will not be with you at all times during your workouts. That said, they should be able to explain things to you on the phone and teach you how to do certain moves without physically being present through every workout.

....

3   **Professionalism –** While it's important to maintain a close relationship of trust, there also needs to be a high level of professionalism throughout the entire process.

....

4   **Education-Knowledgeable –** Coaches should have references and be able to show you their end result for their area of expertise.

....

5   **Personality of Empathy and Compassion but Firm, Fair and Consistent –** As a client, you want to feel comfortable and trust that your coach has your best interest at hand but will not allow you to not ultimately reach your goal.

....

Total Score ....%

CHAPTER 5

Practice, Practice, Practice

Why do I need to Practice, I'm the best in the Neighborhood? When Allen Iverson had the press conference and mentioned the word practice more than (50) times, people started to believe that talent will develop on its own. The saying "Practice makes Perfect" is an accurate statement based on making your child fundamentally sound and proficient in their craft. Frustrated parents, coaches and athletes often confuse support with constantly reminding the children they need to practice more, condition more, concentrate more, etc. Overly involved parents and coaches frequently lose their impartiality. They are unable to provide critical emotional support which children often need before and during highly competitive contests.

Practice in whatever you do in life is the fundamental element of transition. In the arena and levels we advance through in our sports/life journey. Our practice routine will become a vital part of our development. If we are going to practice towards transition how and where we are, then we should strive for mastery at the level of modification we desire. Many will not get to their desired dream, and some may not even essentially wish for mastery, but the objective and visualization of excellence can persuade us to put our best effort forward in our daily practice routine and be fully present and committed to what we are undertaking.

What is Practice and what can it do for you?

A fundamental component of any change process, personal change or developmental change, is in the concept of practice. But what is practice and why is it so important?

Practice is simply the act of doing something over and over again, whether that something is as complicated as doing a public speech for the first time or as simple as taking out the trash on the respective day of pick-up. We call it practice when the undertaking becomes a repeated behavior on an individualized task

Practice can be a time set aside to knowingly focus on practice, such as when we set aside time to practice basketball, meditation, exercise, or singing. When it comes to sports, the definition of the word practice is still unclear in that we are always practicing something, whether we are conscious of it or not. Our daily routines are always being refined. How we behave in team or business meeting, our opinion when it is time to do disagreeable activities in all of these circumstances, we are practicing how we should be, though usually without conscious purpose. Practice, Practice, Practice is always happening. It is continuously sculpting us opening us up to new ways of being, or increasingly solidifying the way we exhibit, perform, and finish.

As a former highly decorated collegiate athlete who thought I was the best thing the sports world had ever witnessed soon came to a screeching halt on a normal January day in Louisiana on the campus of Grambling State University in the year of 1979. As a fairly decorated well-trained and confident track and field athlete leaving high school, I prepared to make my mark on the world at the college level and found myself in the presence of three highly decorated athletes also. As we were introduced and each ones accolades were announced of the participants, I found myself even more confident that I was going to win this race in premier fashion because this is what I had prepared for in all my previous years of practice and preparation. Then the gun went off and all of the realities of what if, came to actuality. What if they were much better than me. What if I hadn't prepared to compete on the highest collegiate level with runners who had taken their practice just as serious as I, or more? What if my first experience with a banked track was not a good experience? What if the fear of losing perpetuated the will to quit? What if this was the true lesson of humility how would that affect my overall attitude towards continuing to compete at this level? In my previous preparation, had I mentally, physically and spiritually been ready to receive this day? Well the end results crushed every bit of confidence I had built up to compete on this level with this caliber of talent. I had put in the work and in my practice sessions I pushed myself to the point of exhaustion and truly believed I was ready. The one thing I learned that day is, as you move towards the highest level of your sport, everyone who competes is the best that they ever did it in that era. There is no coasting, there is no time off, there is no half speed; everything is in game time speed. So, if your practice is at half speed you will react at half speed and your results will be evident of that preparation. Practice in sports is just like life; if you want to be the best your practice must bring the best out of you every time. Some who have made it may disagree with this concept but in every sport or business those who have made their names synonymous with greatness will tell you they never took a play, race, down, goal, swing or day off. Practice makes perfect!!

Activity: The Reflector

This activity is for the resilient only: Ask someone to be a verbal observant mirror, so you can see yourself in action.

Begin by identifying someone to serve as your reflector. The person must be observant, articulate, and secure enough to tell you the truth. And you have to be ready to hear that truth -- and to act on it.

Explain to this person that you want her or him to pay attention to your production for the next three-four weeks. Describe and write down the specific results you are trying to modify and what you hope to accomplish. Then ask for frequent feedback and change action steps.

Bringing a reflector into the process can provide two important benefits: (1) you get useful information in the form of a description of your coaching / training behavior from an outside perspective, and (2) you have increased your investment in the outcome. You are a lot more likely to work on your performance after you have told someone what you are doing.

Learn from what your reflector tells you to improve your coaching / training skills.

26

CHAPTER 6

Expose your child to the historical journey of their sport of preference and the odds they're up against

To know where you're going, you must first know from whence you came. The dream of many high school athletes and their parents is that someday the athlete will enter the lucrative world of professional sports. But many people do not understand just how unlikely a destination this is. Much has already been written about the athlete who, after years of ignoring academics and being passed through classes in high school and college, is left with nothing when the professional dream doesn't work out. It's the athlete who suffers the consequence of finally, finding himself / herself with no *education*, job, or skills. But what about the parent (s) who have no clue about the entire process from middle school to college. What classes should my child be enrolled in? When should they begin taking the ACT-SAT? How can I help them prepare for this testing? What are the NCAA requirements? What are my child chances of really playing or graduating? What happens if my child gets hurt? There are many more questions you should ask, but I would suggest you find or create a support group to have all your questions answered. But while it's easy to blame the athlete for not taking advantage of the educational opportunities presented along the way, many times coaches and parents are also complicit in this outcome, one for the wins, the other for the fame. Remember, everything that glitters is not gold.

Basketball and football, the most visible of high school and college sports, have a very low percentage of athletes who play in high school and then eventually move up to the professional ranks. In men's basketball, for example, there is only a 0.03% chance of a pro career. This means that of the almost 556,844 male, high school senior basketball players only 44 will ever be drafted to play in the NBA after college, and even less after high school. Only 32 women (.02%) out of just over 127,000 female, high school senior players will eventually be drafted. In football the odds are slightly better, with 0.08% or 355 of just over 317,000 college senior or junior players being drafted.

The sport with the most professional opportunities is baseball, with high school players having a 0.60% chance of playing professionally. Though still far less than 1%, the number of opportunities within baseball's professional development system helps to increase this percentage. Baseball drafts about 600 NCAA athletes from the 6700 college seniors each year, a number that is far higher than any other professional sport and which represents a need to feed its large farm system. The numbers are critical to the visual of your chances may be in the competitive nature of your sport of choice. Let's take a look at how many jobs are created each year, about 100,000 with a 20% chance of an increase or decrease. This number doesn't reflect the self-starter —entrepreneur who usually is under the radar until he or she's business in making revenue. But to know the game of sports and life and those who paved the way for you to even have an opportunity is crucial to the humbling of your spirit and character. It is said that your character is revealed when you're alone and you think no one is looking and you reveal your true self. The advancement of the game has taken on many challenges and has sacrificed many names. Your child will only get one chance at making a first impression. The professional ranks are no longer a game; it becomes a business which time waits for no-one and money is the master of movement. Tough truthful conversations can and will only enhance your child's chances for success. So, to be the best parent of an aspiring athlete, familiarize yourself with the journey of those who sacrificed their lives to be called a professional athlete and ask yourself are we built for this expedition?

I recently had a conversation with a group of young ball players about who they patterned their game after. In their opinion, who were the best players to have ever played the game of basketball and football? This conversation took many different twist and turns on how they validated their opinion of who was the best players in both sports. The interesting thing which inspired me to share this was how shallow their knowledge was of who played each sport and how far they couldn't go back and recognize players who had made an impact on their perception of greatness in the sport, versus the impact the player has made as a person. The interesting point of the conversation for me was how each one described a few plays they could recall which made the ESPN highlight reel verses the players work ethic, family commitment, community commitment, or what have they (social media) done lately. I then asked them to define greatness in a sport. Was it how high one could jump? Then Earl "The Goat" Manigault and David Thompson would be defined as great? They didn't know either. Was it how fast one could run? Then John Carlos, Bullet

Bob Hayes and Carl Lewis would be defined as great, a few of them knew one person. Was it ball handling skills? Then Marcus Haynes and Earl the Pearl Monroe, Pistol Pete Maravich would be defined as great. They quickly pulled out their phones and began to Google their answers, because we were still stuck on defining GREAT and what constituted any players name being engraved in the sport conversations of one of the best to have ever played. As they pulled up videos to validate their opinion of why a certain player was and should be in that conversation, it all reverted back to the short snippets displayed on the highlight reels, which resulted in a lot of woos and high fives but in my opinion based on woos, then Deandre Jordon and LeBron James highlight dunks would signify greatness? Our conversation then changed to football because we were at a high school game, but it lasted a whole (10) minutes (lol) because they couldn't go back more than (2) seasons of "Great Players" but had more conversation in reference to the negative behavior, cars, jewelry and social media escapades which dominate their beings, more than the ones who played the sport and didn't let the sport play them. We agreed to disagree that our journeys has given us different experiences and that sports has played a huge part in the development or under-development of our communities based on if you felt that a person was responsible for giving back what was given to him or her in their sports training. We never came to a consensus on the definition of sports greatness, we just agreed on a few players having exceptional talent, some could have even played in different eras and succeeded. But for me, sports greatness is defined by where you stand in the hour of variance because there have been men and women who sacrificed their entire careers because of the injustice defined by the dollar bill. So my question is; do you want to be or raise a professional athlete? First thing in my opinion is, do know who cultivated the land you claim as yours, for you to be able to say "This is the house I built".

Activity

Mind mapping chart starting with your sport or career choice and start from where you are right now (Middle, High, College) and determine who was the best at what they did and what was their journey and habits to success?

CHAPTER 7

**Remind yourself daily of the saying;
"Jack of all trades, master of none" Entering your child in multiple sports could eventually turn your child away from sports all together**

Would you enter your child into (5) different schools because each one in your opinion, had the best curriculum in each subject manner? Developing your son or daughter into an athletic superstar is a long process. As Zen Master/ Former Chicago Bulls, Los Angeles Lakers Head Coach and now New York Knicks General Manager Phil Jackson said it: "There's no percentage in trying to push the river or speed up the harvest. The farmer who's so eager to help his crops grow that he slips out at night and tugs on the shoots inevitably ends up going hungry."

The problem with starting your potential superstar in an under-five league is burnout, frustration and de-motivation. "*The American Academy of Pediatrics (AAP)* asserts that when the demands of a team sport exceed a child's development, the child may become frustrated or believe he or she's a failure." When children quit sports it's because they view themselves as a failure, they typically leave all sports; children who have a positive experience in a sport continue with the sport or have the confidence to try other sports or physical activities. They also excel at other experiences because they have experienced success in their sports experience. Keeping children involved in sports, even at a non-competitive level, is essential to reduce the childhood obesity epidemic, but they must feel a sense of accomplishment.

Unfortunately, "*Three-fourths (75%) of pediatricians surveyed* report that the amount of time their young patients spend on unstructured play has decreased in the past (5) years." Organized youth sports are one of the greatest factors for this decline, which is positive and negative. On the positive side, these children are participating in an active activity and learning the value or teamwork and cooperation in a team setting. On the negative, some organized youth sports often are coached by over-competitive under-achieving individuals who are using this venue to validate their playing experiences or personal short falls in their sports career and often, they ignore the reasons children choose playing sports in the first place: activity, be with friends, learn a skill, have fun, etc.

Rather than creating an environment of play maximizing these attributes of sports, coaches systematically ignore these facts for the winning season. Activity is lessened as children are re-strained by the rules of the game and the additional rules a coach imposes on the players; friends are divided onto different teams; skills go untaught and fun is diminished. Add to this that many children are developmentally unprepared for the demands of sports-especially socially, cognitively and psychologically-and organized sports fail to maximize its potential benefits.

People by nature work hard at something they love to do; by initiating a child in a sport too early, and by playing that sport too much, the child is apt to lose the passion for the game and view practice much like homework, which always has a negative connotation. Instead, parents need to nurture a healthy appreciation for the game and the value of hard work by building self-confidence and creating a safe, fun environment.

When players experiment, they gain a deeper appreciation for their own skills. By building general athletic skills in an uncompetitive environment through free play, the youth athlete is prepared to join a sports team around ten to eleven years old and experience success, even playing with and against others who have been in the competitive mix for several years.

While the general skill acquisition will not translate to immediate improvement in a sport-specific skill, in the long run, a deeper well of general athletic skills provides the foundation for long-term success, even if the results are not immediately evident. Athletics success is a process. And during the journey, the skills developed and the experiences is greater than the destination.

Activity

Chart all sports you or your child is in and determine what's your local, state, national and international rank. Once you determined that, develop a plan of action on what it's going to take for colleges or professional teams to notice you.

Objective
What is your purpose for choosing this event?

Information
Name and place of tournament, also, who will be there to evaluate you or your child's talent?

Verification
Make sure your name is entered or registered in the group who everyone is watching.

Activity
Will this highlight your or your child's true talent?

Results
How did you or your child perform?

Next Event
What next on your agenda?

CHAPTER 8

Find the best competition events for your child to get an accurate account of their true ability

As an Executive Life Coach to professional, college and aspiring athletes as well as educational leaders, business owners, community organizers, celebrities and people who just want to do better in the role of a parent, I have experienced and witnessed through conversations, providing lectures and seminars, leading businesses to growth and financial success, attending sporting events, developing school cultures or just watching sporting events at the local sports bar, the deep craving parents or just spectators have is to see their children triumph in the competitive arena. Whether academic or athletic, there is intensity in their appearance when it comes to competing and winning. In my journey as an educator, I have worked with gifted students, early stage athletes and highly competitive coaches and families. I have concluded that there is something that is far more important than the win/loss record, and more privileged than a sport brand endorsement. I have concluded that a strong and honorable character is more precious and lasting than any athletic glory. It is the character of our young people that parents should pay attention to if they want them to compete at the highest level rather than winding up in the wasteland of losers.

What do I mean by the most unsophisticated consciousness intellect? "Too many early stage athletes get over-trained for their physical ability under the influence of unaccomplished athletes who are living vicariously through their child or student on getting the win, by any means necessary." In my long and rather accomplished career as a youth coach, I would tell our athletes all the time, if you just want to win, go play against someone of lessor skills, but if you want your win to have significance, play against someone who you know you can't beat. If you lose, what did you learn from the outcome? If you're in this game to be the best, the loss builds your buoyancy, commitment, work ethic and your obedience to the game. It also intensifies your ability to get up after being conquered, literally or metaphorically.

Has your child or you ever participated in every aspect of sports in your neighborhood and believed that he / she was the best player ever to lace up a pair of sneakers or spikes? For me, basketball was the only thing that occupied my every thought until I realized the TRUTH; growing up in the Northeast if you believed you had any basketball skills at all you had to take your skills to Rucker Park. I recall believing the summer before I entered high school that my path was already paved for the NBA and the only place you could be truly evaluated was on the court of the Kings. So a few of us jumped on the train and headed to Harlem, basketball in hand and our Chuck Taylors over our shoulders, ready to make our name legendary on the court where stars are born and losers sent home. We never had an opportunity to play but I do remember a young gentleman around 20 years old, walked up with a bottle of wine and asked for the ball; he then without hesitation proceeded to hit (30) jumpers in a row, then saying nothing, picked up his wine bottle and walked away like this was his normal routine. No one seemed amazed or in awe of this feat. This is when I realized, talent is an innate trait about which many of us are in denial when looking at your childs or your own true ability.

The famous Rucker Park was opened on February 23rd 1956 which was first named as P.S. 156 Playground. In 1965, Mr. Rucker, a New York City Parks Department worker, brought his small basketball TP league to the outdoor park after staging his games at several different neighborhood sites. By the 1970's, the spot had grown into the Mecca of street basketball, with so much talent that the Elite (24) of the park, many never knew but the ones who were known changed the game we all know as basketball, included Wilt Chamberlain, Connie Hawkins, Kareem Abdul-Jabbar, Kobe Bryant, Kevin Durant, Kyrie Irving, Rafer "Skip To My Lou" Alston, Nate "The Skate" Archibald, Joe "The Destroyer" Hammond, "Jumpin" Jackie Jackson, Richard "Pee Wee" Kirkland, Herman "Helicopter" Knowlings, Earl "The Goat" Manigault, Conrad "McNasty" McCrae, Earl "The Pearl" Monroe, Calvin Ramsey, Kareem "Best Kept Secret" Reid, Pablo Robertson, Charlie Scott, Frank "Shake N' Bake" Streety, Corey "Homicide" Williams, James "Fly" Williams, James "Speedy" Williams, Larry "Bone Collector" Williams, James "Pookie" Wilson, Sam Worthen Anyone who thought they were someone came to Harlem to play against New York's greatest street players. It was there that a knowing neighborhood population could watch Julius Erving meet his match against Joe Hammond, a playground legend called the Destroyer who never played a minute of high school or college ball. Your talent will never be measured by your neighborhood games in your driveway, neighborhood field or in front of the television or an electronic game; it's who you're exposed to in your talent development that will elevate your confidence and work ethic to be the best player you're capable of being in whatever arena you choose.

Activity: How Relevant Am I?

To "be present" is to interact with other people in a way that minimizes the many obstacles to hearing and understanding what people are really saying and needing. This is a critical element of perception.

The following exercise helps you diagnose what gets in the way of your "Being Relevant".

Rate yourself against each statement on a scale of 1 to 3:

1   *"I rarely or never do this."*

2   *"I do this sometimes."*

3   *"I do this often."*

During conversations, (1)... Assessment

1   Think about what I'm waiting to say next, even while others are still speaking

....

2   Change the subject, for no reason in particular when I don't feel its accurate

....

3   Ignore or discount what others are saying

....

4   Clarify what I hear and see of my own experience, rather than taking it at face value

....

5   Drift or lose focus on the relevancy of the conversation if I feel I'm being attacked

....

6   Silently critique or judge what others say, even while they are still speaking

....

7   Focus only on what others are saying when it interests me

....

8   Focus on special opinions which cause me to lose sight of the main purpose or concerns

....

9   Look for points of disagreement rather than points of agreement

....

10 Know more about the sport than the coach or trainer

....

Add the following scores:

Items 1, 4, and 7; Items 2, 5, and 8; Items 3, 6, and 9 and 10

Each of these three scores indicates how you deal with a different obstacle present in interactions with others. Low scores are better than high scores, and any score of "5" or above indicates an opportunity for improvement.

CHAPTER 9

Inform them of all other sports, and areas related or associated with sports

In many conversations between educators and sports coaches, student-athlete is a taboo word. Most people are told to be one or the other, practice becomes too intense and schools and coaches are pressured to win by any means necessary, so academics in many cases is secondary. Most athletes are attracted to the more exposed sports, but most colleges athletic budgets exceed (50) million dollars and offer at least (20) different male and female sports which offer scholarships and degree opportunities. Many parents may feel that their child has professional aspirations and may not gravitate toward the less-exposed sports, but we all must remember that 2011 student-athletes speech which stated; *"There are over 400,000 NCAA student-athletes, and most of us will go pro in something other than sports."* In reports published by the NCAA, it shows academic graduation rates slowly increasing in some of the major Division I colleges and universities, but we all know, for me to sell my business I must show you the buyer how good my product is. Many coaches have sat in thousands of living and dining rooms and told parents on countless occasions, I'm going to treat your son or daughter just like they were mine. I would then ask them, how many of their children graduated from college and did they play sports or was academics the priority in their household? I ask this question only to bring attention to the end result of your child's college career, academically and athletically. Then we see and hear of all those who didn't make it to the professional ranks and many ask, what would they have done for the game or themselves in the choices they made, if they had had better guidance or direction? Well, maybe if we're true about the numbers of those who make it, as stated in a previous chapter, and not be dream killers, but be realistic about their chance of having a profession-al athletic career, and make sure they're on the road to receiv-ing a degree and or their net-worth has been developed by their network of meeting people who can help the rest of their life be beneficial. Then, with this approach we begin the networking required to expose them to the additional opportunities associated with the sport they love, or once loved. Parents who do this, guide aspiring stars in the right direction and help them see clearly the pitfalls, obstacles, and opportunist which await the elite players. In sports, students must experience extensive career-related discovering activities to earn their true knowledge of how sports can extend their dreams of being connected to the sports, while still making a very good living. Activities may include curiosity assignments, career research, education planning, job shadows, service learning projects, work experience, internships in multiple areas of interest, and class-room projects tied into real life issues. Do your due diligence with your child and learn about every support initiative and prospect for your child to explore and get connected through and then support these efforts. Talk about them with your children. Help make them more than just requirements on a checklist but a road map for their life outcome. Every young person and even many parents refuse to have a conversation about anything but being that professional athlete. They believe anything short of that equals failure. Well, let me let you in on a little secret you can only find here in this guide, **SO YOU WANT TO BE A PROFESSIONAL ATHLETE** There are a lot more people in the world who never played the exposed professional sports than there are who did, but I'm going to give you a second secret complimentary. This business outside of playing is projected to grow to make **$145.3 billion** between the years 2013-2017, and still growing. The sports industry is flourishing with opportunities in multiple global areas including: sports marketing, agents, lawyers, trainers, owners, clothing marketing, supplements, rehabilitation facilities, company sponsorship, sports media (traditional and social media), sports facilities and even higher education institutions which are growing faster than average projected rate of 15% just to name a few. You do the math, an average sports career last (3-5 years) 78% end up in some type of financial hardship after their playing days are over, the average life expectancy is (75-85) years of age, more money, more money, and more money. Please don't get me wrong, to have my jersey and name mentioned with the best who ever played would be electrifying, but again you do the math. Who was the team that finished seconded last year in the NBA Championship, WNBA Championship, Super Bowl, World Series, World Cup, and NHL Championship? But one thing is consistent the name's on the world's most wealthy list.

Activity: Family Road Trip (College, Professional, Music, Professional Careers) Hall of Fames, Museums

American football

- College Football Hall of Fame
- Green Bay Packers Hall of Fame
- Pro Football Hall of Fame
- New Orleans Saints Hall of Fame

Association football

- English Football Hall of Fame
- Gwladys Street's Hall of Fame
- National Soccer Hall of Fame (U.S.)
- Norwich City F.C. Hall of Fame
- Scottish Football Hall of Fame
- Brazilian Football Museum Hall of Fame

Basketball

- Australian Basketball Hall of Fame (formerly NBL Hall of Fame)
- FIBA Hall of Fame
- Greek Basketball Hall of Fame
- Indiana Basketball Hall of Fame (U.S.)
- Naismith Memorial Basketball Hall of Fame (U.S.)
- National Collegiate Basketball Hall of Fame (U.S.)
- Women's Basketball Hall of Fame

Baseball and softball

- ⊙ Canadian Baseball Hall of Fame
- ⊙ Cuban Baseball Hall of Fame
- ⊙ Irish American Baseball Hall of Fame (U.S.)
- ⊙ Japanese Baseball Hall of Fame
- ⊙ Mexican Baseball Hall of Fame
- ⊙ National Baseball Hall of Fame and Museum (U.S.)
- ⊙ National College Baseball Hall of Fame (U.S.)
- ⊙ Atlanta Braves Museum and Hall of Fame
- ⊙ Boston Red Sox Hall of Fame
- ⊙ Cincinnati Reds Hall of Fame
- ⊙ Cincinnati Reds Hall of Fame and Museum
- ⊙ Kansas City Royals Hall of Fame
- ⊙ New York Mets Hall of Fame
- ⊙ New York Yankees Monument Park
- ⊙ Philadelphia Baseball Wall of Fame
- ⊙ St. Louis Cardinals Hall of Fame Museum
- ⊙ Seattle Mariners Hall of Fame
- ⊙ National Softball Hall of Fame (U.S.)

Ice hockey

- ⊙ Hockey Hall of Fame
- ⊙ IIHF Hall of Fame
- ⊙ United States Hockey Hall of Fame
- ⊙ Wisconsin Hockey Hall of Fame

CHAPTER 10

Make sure there is balance and order in their / your life

"The true treasures in life are not what you have materialized in the end, but how many prospered along the journey with you." The probability of achieving lasting fame and glory via sports is controlled. Many have, but many more have not. There is a quote I said earlier in the book which I use every day. It states; "The reputation of a thousand years can be determined (destroyed) by the conduct of one hour." In a society which only remembers your last basket, touchdown, home run, goal, world record time, throw, jump or qualifying lap, it's your name and character which live on forever. I remember entering high school wanting to play basketball, because basketball was all that I lived for, but it didn't work out for me for various reasons, so my life-long friend Michael Jones suggested that since I was going to run track later in the year, maybe I should join him running cross-country. I told him, he had to be crazy because first, the race was over three miles and that Coach Black had them training every day, running about ten (10) miles. He said don't worry we'll just coast so as we prepared for the indoor and

49

outdoor season, we did just that, never coming in last but real close to last until the first meet was scheduled. Coach Black would bring us all in the (war room) and strategize how we were going to win each meet; he would write down each event at the meet and who would or should score what points. Well Mike and I were lucky just to be in the varsity race let alone called on to score any points. As we arrived at the park where the race was to take place, I saw a few other people from different teams warming up talking about who was who from each school and who they had to beat or at least stay in touch with and try to take over at the end of the race. I then said to Michael "Why aren't they talking about beating us?" he said "Because they know we will do our thing indoor and outdoor track, we're just getting in shape for that season now". Well, for me that wasn't a good enough answer, I lived and slept in the same house as an Olympian, I always wanted to win at everything I did or at least let you know I was in the building and lastly my father told me I was an Edwards first. Now to many what does that mean? For me, it meant you're not just representing yourself, there a long list who carry this name and you better carry it well! Shortly, in the book I'll state my father said all he could give me was his name and so in Track and Field my brother had made that name something to stand up and respect and you can bet your last dollar I was not going to let the name down. As the race began, we all lined up according to your status on the team. Mike and I on the back line and the gun went off, so we did what we always did in practice, just enough until people started to pull away and I asked him, was this for real and he said yes but they don't expect us to score and I said but they can't beat me!!! I took off, and I remember him saying go ahead but pace yourself. My pride to win never let me pace myself; it fueled me to win at any cost. As the race progressed, people began laughing at me on how I was running so fast to be in a cross country race and as I went by them, they said you're going to burn yourself out. Well that happened but the others in the race were also beginning to burn out, so I was thinking, If I'm in front of you, you'll have to catch me. As we came around the last stretch of the race and I saw people in my sight, I remember the other teams saying in the beginning on how to run the race, and they said, if you keep him close you can take them in the end. That fueled me even more, my mind was like you were going to respect the name Edwards every time I walk out here at a meet. In the end I finished 7th overall in a race I was never supposed to compete in, let alone score points. As I crossed the finish line, I remember almost falling in the pond because I was so exhausted and no-one even noticed because they thought it was a mistake and I had cut the course and cheated. When the marshals all checked in, the first thing I remember hearing them ask, had I cut through the park to win 7th place and they said no, he was running possessed, he ran past every check point. This is when they said, Edwards how did you do that, what a great race. But from that day on, I made sure everyone knew it was my pride that would not let me have to go home and say I lost with a chance to win but that my work ethic determined my outcome. Which has the lasting/legacy memory? My track and field career from that day forward never took a back seat to anyone except Me!!!. To this day I remember my father telling me that he didn't have a lot of material things to leave me, so all he could leave me with was his name and that was all his father could leave him. All your worldly possessions will remain here for someone to cherish, or in many cases sell for monetary gain. Everyone who is blessed with life has a great opportunity to contribute to the betterment of mankind. If your passion or path of contribution is not sports, find your lane and run in it unapologetically with the pride, confidence and vigor that no one can or will ever do it better than you. Why? Some do make it to stardom, and will make their name synonymous with the sport they played forever; it could be you. One out of every hundred-thousand high school athletes becomes a professional athlete. Why can't it be your son, daughter or you? Although many young athletes never achieve professional status, their sports experiences enabled them to develop lifelong values, relationships, team work and self-respect of losing and winning in the game of life which last much longer than your greatest sports moment. Make your child's or your journey one of charitable memorable moments for which they would not trade for all the money in the world. When it is all said and done for me and please believe, there are a few days I wish I could have back, my hope is, that those who met me or competed against me during my athletic / life journey, truly believe I was an extraordinary athlete. However, my wish would be to be known as a much better Producer, Provider, Protector, Father, Grandfather, Inspirational Speaker, Comedian, Community Activist, Educator, Entrepreneur, Sports Coach, Consultant, Life Coach, but ultimately A TRUE MAN of the CREATOR.

Activity: Personal Life Chart

Do a personal self-evaluation of your life choices, and ask yourself, has this put you in the best place you should or could be right now?

Topic	Current Situation	Hours per week	Future Objectives
Health How important is your health to you?			
Wealth Define wealth and how will you get to your goal?			
Family What and who are important?			
Relationships Are they important and with who?			
Contribution What is yours and is it enough?			
Spiritual What is your walk and how important is this in your life?			
Leisure/Balance What does fun look like?			
Lack of What other areas of your life need your attention?			

Reflections on my time spent with Coach Rory Edwards in the mid-eighties

There are three proven investments this every aspiring athlete needs from their coach if they are going to be successful in their chosen sport and more importantly later in life. They are confidence, relationship and time.

Coach Edwards invested in me a proper understanding of confidence. A proper understanding of confidence was very critical because as a young athlete I had talents and gifts, but my misplaced confidence in those talents and gifts matured into arrogance and a sense of entitlement in competition. Coach Edwards was instrumental in reorienting my thinking and demonstrating that proper confidence emanates from a partnership between coach and athlete. Coach Edwards was able to get the best out of me in practice so when it came time to perform I was in the best position to succeed, not because of talents and gifts alone. Coach Edwards instilled in me a different root source for my confidence which was more aligned with why he was so confident in me. My confidence shifted from my talents and gifts to the fact that I knew I was one of the best prepared athletes competing on that day. Consequently, when I lacked confidence after a defeat or in facing a bigger, stronger and faster opponent I knew that whatever the outcome was I could say I paid the price in practice to compete.

The second investment Coach Edwards made was embracing the reality that we were in a relationship as coach and athlete that was forged because of sports, but not limited to sports. I was the product of a single mother home and Coach Edwards realized that I needed male mentoring in addition to athletic training. He understood there were some off the field realities that I faced that influenced and shaped part of what drove me in sports. He didn't compartmentalize our relationship and focus solely on my athletic development, but my personal development as well. Every athlete has familial challenges and many athletes are driven to sports as a way to escape from or address those challenges in their life. A coach by default becomes a mentor whether they choose to be or not. What I mean is every coach will teach their athlete something about life that will outlast the bond they presently share due to sports. For this reason, grown men and women still refer to their coaches as "Coach" long after their competitive days are over both as a sign of respect and an indication of perpetual relationship.

Differing athletes will have differing relationships with their coach based on their needs as individuals and the coach's ability to give of him or herself. Some athletes need more "coach" than "mentor" in the relationship or vice-versa. Some athletes may need to be coached up one day and encouragingly patted on the back another day. Some athletes will become more coachable when they know you are in a mentoring relationship with them. Coach Edwards by embracing the totality of who I was and what I needed as a human being created a harmonious balance between coach and mentor. He was a father figure and nurturer when I needed one, but also was a coach and authority figure when I needed that. To coach an athlete means entering into a personal relationship with those athletes and the quality of that relationship will greatly impact the performance in the competitive arena. I competed for myself, but I also competed for Coach Edwards because I knew he cared about the totality of my personhood and we were partners in a relationship that was not limited to sports.

Finally, Coach Edwards made the investment of time. Developing an athlete especially those with professional potential takes time. Time on the practice field or in the venue of competition is understood and interpreted by most coaches and athletes as time well spent. There is another aspect of time, equal to if not more valuable that I recall spending with Coach Edwards. The time I spent with him where the focus wasn't on practice or competition, but on life or character building. Coach Edwards used time with me away from the specter of sports to teach me lessons about living while not in competition. He was a coach who established that we needed time to prepare and practice for athletic competition, but also time to prepare and practice for the competition of life. Coach Edwards was focused on training an athlete; however, he never lost sight of using some time he spent with me to prepare me for days in the future when competition would no longer be possible. These times together away from practice or in periods of transportation to and from competition were invaluable because the discussions were not about sports, but manhood, character, landmines in life and personhood. As the joy of winning those competitive contests and the stings of defeat have faded with time, what I now reflect on is those moments in time where I know he was preparing me to win at life, win as a father, win as a man and win as a husband.

John L. Smith, Pastor, Father of Three, Husband to Melonie and former State and New England Champion in Track and Field

Top Twenty-One Jobs projected in the next (10) ten years – Our network of Professional's can align you with your Career Mentor

1	Sales representative/business developer
2	Software designer/developer
3	Doctors / Nurse
4	Accounting & finance executive and staff
5	Networking/systems administrator
6	Administrative assistants
7	Business analyst (software implementation)
8	Business analyst (research)
9	Financial developer
10	Educator
11	Project manager
12	Testing/quality assurance
13	Database administrator
14	Technology executive
15	Electrical / Mechanical engineer
16	Sports industry
17	Government contracts administrator
18	Judicial / probation officers
19	Attorney / Para legal
20	Marketing Specialist
21	Biomechanical Engineer

About the Author

For more than (25) twenty-five years, Rory T. Edwards has established himself as an internationally recognized leader and innovator in the world of education, athletic wellness and lifestyle transformation. Mr. Edwards is also Founder and President of Professional Athletes' Wellness Group. Our mission is to be regarded as the most effective resource for enabling stability, longevity, and wellness into the lives of professional and aspiring athletes transitioning towards financial prosperity and international popularity.

As a Father, Grandfather, Community Activist, Educator, Entrepreneur, Sports Coach, Consultant, Comedian, Motivational / Inspirational Speaker and LIFE COACH. He has always been very interested and have spent many years researching, how children and adults understand and respond to misfortune in their lives. He confidently believes that one's response to failure or to the possibility of failure is a strong indication of a person's internal sense of self-worth and feelings of competence and value. His passion to bridge the access and resource gap for underserved youth runs deep and he knows that sports can be that vehicle. He states: "The devastation of an empire begins in the heart of the young, the astuteness of the adults, in the eyes of the old, but essentially in the language of its citizens."

Rory T. Edwards is available for workshops, seminars and speaking engagements. Or to book Rory T. Edwards, you can contact, M. Patrice Group / Melanie Calloway / office 704.280.8322 or log on to his website @ *www.rorytedwards.com* or send an email @ *rorytedwards1@gmail.com*

For additional copies of the book, "So you want to be a Professional Athlete" you can order them online @ *www.rorytedwards.com* or send an email @ *rorytedwards1@gmail.com* for a personal autographed copy.